I'VE GOT YOUR BACK!

Respecting the Irreplaceable
Executive Assistant

Moriah Freeman
Illustrated by Sarah
Faith Spencer

Kindle Direct Publishing

ISBN-13: 9798722992956
ISBN-10: 1477123456

Cover Design by Moriah Freeman
Cover Photo by Shutterstock
Illustrations by Sarah Faith Spencer
Author Photo by David Vogt
Library of Congress Control Number: 2018675309
Printed in the United States of America

Dedication

**To the many incredibly talented
Executive Assistants (EAs) with whom I have worked.**

ENDORSEMENTS FOR "I'VE GOT YOUR BACK!"

~~~~~~~~

Reading "I've Got Your Back, Respecting the Irreplaceable Executive Assistant" prompted me to reflect more specifically on the Executive/Executive Assistant partnerships I have observed in the universities and governing boards in my experience. The book provides an excellent lens on the E/EA partnership model. Its discussion of desired key features reveals various sources of the model's effectiveness, including nuanced mutual understanding, openness for individual creativity, and support for comity, flexibility, and resilience, as a team and individually.

Freeman's book has wide applicability for many types of organizations, for a variety of positions, and for different stages of development of both individuals and organizations. It will be a valuable guide/resource for individuals in partnerships as they navigate together to address multiple or conflicting needs, encounter unexpected obstacles, sort choices among competing priorities and personalities, wrestle with limits on their time, energy, resources, and discover that they play the roles of both "server" and "served".

I especially value the author's alerting readers to how Executive Assistants can supplement their direct communications with Executives by quiet, unobtrusive observations of the Executives ways in various situations. The Assistants' derived and more nuanced understanding of the Executives in their shared sphere, holds much promise that their individual and collaborative effectiveness will be expedited and enhanced. Freeman's recurring focus on respect, interpersonal caring and understanding, incorporation of core values, and her insightful suggestions for E/EA partnerships are powerfully persuasive that all of these are integral to the quality of the E/EA bond. The book's emphasis on these elements also elevates the potential of the E/EA partnership model itself. Perhaps the author is giving readers an implicit invitation and encouragement to apply them in other relationships, and more broadly in life where better partnerships are much needed.

—Linda S. Wilson
President Emerita, Radcliffe College

~~~~~~~

Moriah Freeman's book on the crucial role Executive Assistants (EAs) play in the smooth running of organizations is a superb compendium of her remarkable insights into the many human facets of the position. Each chapter captures, in a compelling way, her deep understanding of the complexity of the position in all its dimensions. From "Anticipation and Prescience" to "Complementarity" to "Political Savvy and Diplomacy" to "Reliability and Loyalty" to learning from "Failure" to "Transitioning to New Leadership," she explores the ways that EAs are "irreplaceable." They are key enabling partners of the Executive. I believe the book should be read not only by EAs but also by Executives. Moriah Freeman's years of experience serving as an EA during the transition of Radcliffe College to an Institute of Advanced Study at Harvard to her role in supporting me at Harvard as Dean of what is now the John A. Paulson School of Engineering and Applied Sciences have given her a unique and wide-ranging perspective to write this very insightful book.

—Venky Narayanamurti, Emeritus Professor and former
Dean, Harvard University

~~~~~~~~

"I've Got Your Back!" offers an engaging portrayal of the transformative power of a true partnership between an Executive and her Executive Assistant. This book is an invaluable asset for both leaders and those who support them. Moriah Freeman illuminates the Executive Assistant's often invisible role in making an organization function seamlessly, sharing insightful advice from decades of experience on the front lines.

—Oliver Caplan, Composer and Artistic & Executive Director of Juventas New Music Ensemble

~~~~~~~

A strong Executive Assistant/Executive partnership

can double or triple an executive's output and success. The strong partnership can help an organization successfully weather difficult times and promote stability during dynamic changes. However, an executive who doesn't value their assistant or an assistant who doesn't value themselves can squander this potential treasure. Moriah Freeman's text "I've Got Your Back" is a valuable resource for executives and their assistants. Ms. Freeman's expertise, earned over 25 years in high-profile offices, is a treasure in itself.

—Corinne Espinoza, Former Executive Assistant, Founder of Good Bank, and Associate Director, Cambridge Economic Opportunity Committee

CONTENTS

I'VE GOT YOUR BACK!

INTRODUCTION

For 23 years of my 25-year career at Radcliffe College and Harvard University, I worked as an administrative or executive assistant (EA). I served a vice president, a president, and multiple deans. While doing so, I worked with executive assistants across the university, at other higher education institutions, in businesses, foundations, government departments and agencies, and at the White House.

After many years of experience, I am disappointed to acknowledge that most executives have no idea what their assistants do behind the scenes to make their offices run smoothly, protect and prop them up, and enhance their effectiveness. A disciplined, committed, experienced, and wise EA can be a leader's or executive's most precious resource. But the executive must recognize the potential of the relationship and respect what the EA has to offer.

A true **partnership** between executive and EA is rare, in my experience. Nevertheless, such a partnership is the aspiration of many career EAs who see their talents as adding value to their principal's leadership skills and accomplishments and who derive a great deal of satisfaction in doing so. They are not unambitious, but while most do not aspire to leadership positions, they have a keen sense of what it takes to make a good leader, and they foster and support leadership qualities in their executives.

Many of these chapters first appeared as posts in my blog entitled "With All Due Respect." After twelve such posts, I realized there were more angles on the EA role than might interest a general blog readership. At the urging of an editor friend, I began to consider expanding the topic into a small niche publication directed toward EAs and their principals.

What is a "**principal**"? "A person who has controlling authority or who is in a leading position...a chief...a CEO." More specifically, a principal is "one who engages another to act as an agent subject to general control or instruction...the person from whom an agent's authority derives." [Merriam-Webster Dictionary]

An **executive assistant** supports an executive or principal.

> An executive assistant is seen as the face of an organization and is someone who provides high-level administrative support to executives in a company or corporation. Like secretaries or personal assistants, they conduct clerical work. However, executive assistants have additional responsibilities and higher levels of tasks to perform that can have an effect on the success or profitability of a business. They may even be asked to represent the executive they support in a meeting or other communications. Executive assistants must be highly organized and be able to prioritize work, have good interpersonal and communication skills, and possess managerial abilities. (https://www.careerexplorer.com/careers/executive-assistant/)

An "executive" exercises administrative or managerial control. Such a person is responsible for managing an organization's affairs and has the authority to make decisions within specified boundaries.

An executive assistant, or EA, supports a person in a leadership role within an organization. *Execute*, the verb, and *executive*, the noun, both apply to the EA. The noun *executive* describes the type of person supported. The verb *execute* describes the kind of activities the assistant performs—executing, on behalf of leaders, plans or decisions that they have developed.

A skilled executive assistant must possess the following: organizational skills; technical abilities, especially computer software familiarity; travel and event planning experience; research capability; financial skills, certainly expense tracking and reimbursement, but also budget development and monitoring; information management and preservation expertise; writing competence for correspondence, reports, and memos; supervisory or management skills if there are others in the office; and the ability to understand the entire organization and be a liaison between the leader and others, including sometimes acting as his or her representative. Also, a current catchphrase in most EA job descriptions is the ability to "multitask," which means the applicant must be able to work very quickly, juggle many "task" balls at once, and remain calm while doing so. A tall order, wouldn't you agree?

Many executive assistants begin their careers in entry-level positions supporting lower-level managers and acquire more extensive skills as their manager's responsibilities grow. Experience qualifies them for higher-level positions. Many refine their expertise through continuing education or workplace development programs, and some eventually move into management positions themselves because of their exceptional performance as assistants.

I have gone into such detail about an EA's work to demonstrate that intelligent, disciplined, hardworking, skilled people (mostly women) are successful in this role. During my EA career, I have seen excellent assistants deeply respected by those they served, as well as extremely talented ones who were considered entirely expendable by their principals. Busy executives sometimes have no clear idea of or appreciation for how much their EAs do behind the scenes to support them.

This book is addressed to EAs and their executives and aims to elucidate many of the intangible qualities that premier executive assistants demonstrate in their support roles. These qualities indicate that they have far more to offer than the lower-level support functions that many executives have come to expect from them. I want to demonstrate the potential for a genuinely productive and rewarding partnership between the mature, experienced EA and her principal.

I also want to describe some of the dilemmas and predicaments that EAs face in workplace culture—a culture sometimes devoid of respect for the value of loyal, long-term, experienced, and reliable employees.

I have worked closely with 30 or so EAs and have the highest respect for what they offer. They are, indeed, in many instances, "the power behind the throne," in the most positive sense. They do their work quietly, often secretly, to promote their executives' success and that of the organizations they serve.

NOTE: I will mostly use the personal pronoun *she* **when referring to an EA. Most executive assistants are women, though I acknowledge that some men do pursue this career. The qualities I will write about apply**

to both male and female EAs. When writing about an executive, I will use *he* and *she* interchangeably.

I. INSIGHT

A s an executive and leader, you may not know that your EA is watching you all the time. She studies your behavior in every situation. She examines your motivations and preferences. She is interested in what makes you happy, frustrated, satisfied, and angry. She watches your habits and listens for hints about your moods. She scrutinizes your beliefs about the world in general and especially about the workplace and your colleagues. Her focus on learning who you are, what you need, and what you expect is intense.

She will observe you subtly, quietly, and diplomatically. You will not even realize she is scrutinizing you, and you will not feel threatened by an invasion of your privacy. An accomplished executive assistant may know you better than you know yourself. She can anticipate your thoughts, reactions, and courses of action. These qualities make her one of your most valuable assets. She cultivates insight into who you are, how you behave, and what you want to accomplish to provide you the highest quality of support and service. The focus, depth of concentration, and attentiveness to minute details that develop this insight are skills she offers in service to you and the advancement of your goals. Respect and value them as essential components of your partnership.

For instance, her insight into your priorities enables her to manage your time, avoid interruptions, and help you accomplish your goals. Her understanding will guide her as she makes appointments, shuffles meetings, and carves out the time you need to breathe, think, write, and plan. All this will happen in the background, perhaps without you giving direction or guidance. You will feel confident in the unspoken understanding between you. That understanding will help you to relax and feel assurance in your interactions with other colleagues. You will be productive and be viewed as an essential contributor to your organization, in part because you know she's got your back.

While she is studying you, she will also examine the organization you both serve. She will seek to understand its priorities and goals; she will have insight into the social atmosphere, any hierarchy that exists, who the critical players and stakeholders are, and their preferences and habits. These insights can guide and balance your own. Rely on them and respect them. Encourage her to offer them to strengthen your partnership.

Not all executive assistants can develop such depth of insight. It takes maturity, skill, practice, and patience. If the EA does not focus on gaining insight into you and your organization, she will find her job harder, and you will find her less helpful in navigating workplace systems and politics.

Your EA's insight will enable her to respect you, and you, her. You are partners.

II. ANTICIPATION OR PRESCIENCE

N othing gave me more satisfaction as an executive assistant than anticipating what my boss would require before she asked for it. On several occasions, she would call out from her office, "I need such-and-such," and I could respond, "I just e-mailed it to you." Her exclamation, "Excellent!" made my heart jump for joy. Those moments of harmony and a sense of partnership were valuable to both of us. They cemented the feeling that we were in this together.

There is no magic in this anticipation or foresight. The EA's prescience is not that of a soothsayer. Instead, it is a skill honed by an in-depth study of the person she is serving and the circumstances at hand. Experience and the desire to make the executive's work life as effective as possible contribute to prescience. But there is another element to foresight: intuition—the "gut feeling" sharpened by the cultivation of awareness and concentration.

Travel itinerary preparation is a perfect example of the value of foresight. While making travel arrangements and preparing an itinerary may seem like a straightforward and simple task, it is an exercise in paying attention to the minutest details of the traveler's preferences and expectations. For what airlines does he have frequent flier memberships? How will departure and arrival times affect his personal life and work? How does he prefer to travel to the airport, and how soon does he want to leave the office to ensure he has plenty of time for security and boarding? Is he a last-minute person or a plenty-of-time person? Where does she prefer to sit on the airplane, and why? What kind of hotel does she like? Have all the registrations been made for the conference she is attending? Are there auxiliary meetings to be scheduled in the city or country she is visiting? What kinds of advance materials does she need, and are they included in the travel briefing folder? How do time differentials affect any conference calls scheduled during the trip? How quickly does she recover from jet lag? It can take months to years to learn the traveler's preferences and needs. The above is only a small sample of the kind of detail the EA internalizes to lay a clean, polished, and complete itinerary before her boss at the exact moment he or she needs it before departure. Once internalized, of course, this kind of detailed anticipation becomes second nature, even rote, perhaps, for the executive assistant.

Highly developed intuitive anticipation, however, is a different matter. It comes into play, for example, when a staff member, or perhaps an executive's peer, walks into the office with a problem. If the EA knows her executive well, she will intuit if this is a problem he will want to deal with immediately, even welcoming an interruption. Or is the issue something that, for various good reasons, he will want to delay? Will the assistant handle the situation respectfully and sensitively? Can she anticipate her boss's reactions and motivations? Is her intuition sharpened and a reliable tool in a wide variety of circumstances?

Anticipation is fifty percent preparation and fifty percent intuition. Honed by learning from one's mistakes, prescience requires constant awareness and concentration. It is one of the executive assistant's most valuable skills.

III. DISCRETION AND CONFIDENTIALITY

O ne of the most commonly required qualities listed in Executive Assistant (EA) position descriptions is "the ability to handle highly sensitive material and information with discretion and confidentiality."

This requirement seems like a no-brainer to anyone who has worked in a business environment. Secrets abound and are indiscreetly shared daily, damaging morale, team dynamics, and sometimes the bottom line. An EA's ability to keep a secret <u>for</u> her boss or <u>from</u>

her boss is invaluable.

Because she is a party to many high-level management confidences, the executive assistant's position in the organization may be a lonely one. Her peers may choose not to share work problems with her for fear she will pass the information on to her boss. And she can communicate little about her work, her opinions, and her dilemmas with her associates without compromising the confidentiality expected by her boss. Loneliness, in this instance, is the price paid for professionalism.

If her executive trusts her, she may have access to his voice mail, e-mail accounts, credit cards, social security number, bank accounts, and other highly sensitive information of both a business and personal nature. As people come and go from his office, she will also see and hear things that reveal very delicate situations and decisions. She is expected not to share this information and sometimes not even to acknowledge awareness of it. In a sense, she is like the butler standing by at a family dinner. She hears all the family secrets and sees them at their best and worst but must keep these insights to herself. Hopefully, the difference for the EA is that the head of the "family" respects her role and knows that the more information she has, the better she can assist him or her.

If she respects her EA, the executive will encourage her to contribute insights gleaned from watching and listening in sensitive situations. Those insights may bring another valuable perspective to the decision-making process. Her view may help the executive better understand the complexities and nuances of workplace issues. The executive will also ensure that her EA fully understands her decisions and openly discusses any opinion differences. Such transparency builds trust and encourages loyalty.

The EA must develop keen intuition about when or whether to share with her boss sensitive information that she has learned from other employees. Her first loyalty is to her principal and to foster his or her effectiveness as a manager and leader. She will know when sharing information is essential and when it is gratuitous. She will be careful not to make confidences and then break them.

As I write, I am aware that I am describing two persons with integrity. The work and the relationship can go badly wrong when one of the parties (executive or assistant) acts dishonestly. Mutual respect and understanding are crucial. Any wonder that an executive worth his salt would put the phrase "the ability to handle highly sensitive material and information with discretion and confidentiality" in his assistant's job description.

IV. STRESS, EQUANIMITY, AND A SENSE OF HUMOR

Why would an executive assistant's job be stressful? Isn't it just a matter of typing most of the day and doing routine tasks like making appointments and booking flights and hotels? Don't EAs have it easy compared to their executives—less pressure, fewer decisions to make? They just do as they are instructed, right?

Wrong! Imagine this. Your boss's calendar is already full of vitally important meetings when you receive a call from the CEO's office asking to schedule an urgent two-hour conference call for "sometime the following day"—the exact time to be determined later. You must clear that day on your principal's calendar and hold it open until further notice. Your boss is at an off-site (the latest jargon for a planning day away from the office). She is unplugged from technology, so you can't consult her to determine who to reschedule and cancel. So, as an experienced, knowledgeable, intuitive EA, you set to work rearranging everything. This change will affect perhaps an entire month of meetings. Each person (or their EA) must be e-mailed or called in priority order. You will have to wait for responses before contacting the next individual or group.

You must put all plans for your workday on hold while you "pivot" to tackle this unexpected rescheduling project. You will call into play your knowledge of your boss's preferences and priorities. You must also be sensitive to the needs and feelings of those you are canceling or rescheduling. You must have developed an excellent working relationship with *their* EAs. You are required to accomplish this project quickly and efficiently while being constantly interrupted by others. You are trusted to keep your cool, have confidence in yourself and your relationship with your boss, smooth ruffled feathers, and diplomatically explain the reason for this change. You may even have to cancel travel plans at the last minute and keep track of the financial implications of doing so. And, in the midst of this, you must remain calm and cheerful, juggling multiple balls with faultless skill and perfect poise.

By the end of the day, you have made significant progress, but you are stressed and exhausted. You realize that, unknowingly, you have been holding your breath all day. Before the workday ends, you receive a call from the CEO's office that plans have changed, and the CEO is delaying the crucial meeting until the following week.

Do you cry? Do you scream? Do you throw your mouse at the wall? No. You sigh, shake your head, and pack up to leave the office. Changes in plans are no surprise. This sort of thing has happened multiple times before. You'll deal with it tomorrow. Perhaps you'll stay on an hour or two to catch up on the work you had planned for the day just passed: pay some bills, reimburse some travel expenses, proofread a report, get a head start on arranging an upcoming trip. Perhaps you'll walk down the hall to chat with a fellow EA about the day, and you'll laugh together to release some of the tension. After all, the day was relatively typical. It could have been worse.

I'm tempted to leave it at this and draw some conclusions now about the qualities of poise and humor exhibited by a top-notch EA. Still, I feel compelled to tell an even more stressful story—the responsibility of being "in between."

An angry employee calls to say he needs to see your boss

immediately. Your principal has widely disseminated an open-door policy. She wants to welcome and listen to others in the organization. But you know the situation with this employee, and you know your boss has already discussed the employee's concerns with him several times. There are plans in the works to address these issues, but they are not yet fully developed. Today your boss has blocked off a couple of hours to work on a critical report and has said she doesn't want to be interrupted. All of this runs through your mind as the employee demands an immediate meeting and says he'll be arriving in five minutes, despite your protests.

You calculate that your boss will welcome an interruption from you in this case, so you quietly enter her office. You inform her that the employee will arrive any minute, and she should stay closeted in the room until further notice; you will handle the situation. She gives you a grateful look; there is complete understanding between you. You close the door and return to your desk.

A few moments later, the employee arrives, red-faced and shouting. You speak softly and offer a relaxed demeanor, trying to mirror the kind of behavior you would like him to exhibit. You explain that your boss is not available now, but you know she is working on the employee's concerns. She will be in touch as soon as she has developed plans. You ask the employee to sit down and explain his objections further while you take notes. You want him to know he is being heard and taken seriously. As he talks, he calms down, and you gently communicate that you are in the middle of a project but that, as soon as you can, you will inform your boss about the conversation that has just occurred. You stand up, the listening session is over, and he departs. You prepare a brief e-mail to your boss, low priority, to communicate any new information or nuances you have just gained. She will read it when she has finished the report, or she'll check with you on the way out to her next meeting. She has complete confidence that you have handled the situation appropriately and may say thank you or may just accept your talents as an intermediary with silent gratefulness.

You sigh, take some deep breaths—another uncomfortable situation defused—and go back to your project. But later, you notice how tired you are, how tight your shoulders. A slight headache hovers around your temples. Perhaps tonight you will go to the gym, listen to your favorite soothing music during your commute, or enjoy a delicious dinner cooked by your understanding spouse.

I have watched many talented EAs keep their composure during extremely stressful incidents. They relate delicate situations that they have handled quietly to prevent them from escalating, saving their boss time, effort, and stress. They understand that their role is sometimes to smooth troubled waters and always to remain flexible, changing projects on a dime in response to their boss's and others' needs. They feel the stress these situations create, but, for the most part, they do not show it. They welcome interruptions with a smile and stay late to finish tasks that have been pushed aside during business hours. They do their best to maintain a sense of humor about themselves and those they serve. Sometimes these efforts at equanimity fray slightly and take a physical toll, but these EAs try to maintain a life balance that keeps them healthy and productive.

None of this differs from the lives of countless workers at all levels in all jobs and professions. I write about it here because I admire the EAs with whom I have shared such stresses. I respect their backstage brilliance, strength, and dedication. We may commiserate in private, but in public, we strive to be models of calm professionalism. If you have such an executive assistant, she or he is worth her or his weight in gold.

V.
COMPLEMEN-
TARITY

The wise leader will know his or her strengths and weaknesses and surround him or herself with a team that will enhance his talents and offset her liabilities. Hiring an EA, like other hires, should therefore be an exercise in complementarity. Likewise, an EA who hopes to bring all of her skills and talents to bear in the position will seek to discover her executive's strong suits as well as shortcomings and will pay careful attention to the areas where she may add needed value to the relationship.

Complementary means "combining in such a way as to enhance or emphasize the qualities of each other or another." [Oxford Dictionaries] The EA will draw out the best qualities in her boss and deflect his deficiencies or supply what is needed in situations where the executive does not shine.

For example, a visionary executive excels at seeing the changes necessary to put her organization on a robust future footing. She may intuit the path required to reach the desired goal and create an ingenious broad-brush plan for leading an institution forward, but she will turn to others on her team to flesh out a detailed strategy. The visionary leader may be blind to road-blocks, pitfalls, and inherent resistance, or, though capable of the vision, may be incapable of inspiring those who must carry it out.

A well-rounded skill and quality set is ideal for a leader, executive, or manager, but I have seldom encountered one who possessed everything necessary to lead well. A visionary leader may be a quiet and uncharismatic person who partners with those who subscribe to his vision and have the charisma to convince and motivate others. A charismatic CEO may rely on his detail-oriented and well-organized executive assistant to ensure he does not miss something critical to his plan's success. He may also trust her to manage his time so he doesn't get lost in side alleys, miss deadlines, or lose sight of the intricacies of what he is trying to accomplish.

Some may not see the importance of complementarity between an executive and her assistant. By comparison, the necessity of a complementary relationship with other teammates or direct reports may seem more pronounced. Let me bring it down to where the "rubber meets the road," so to speak—the classic case of the disorganized leader and the super-organized EA.

This executive does not have to worry about or devote energy to how he will get from A to B or whether he will be on time and well-briefed to meet the challenge when he gets there. He is free to perform in his comfort range to accomplish his goals. His EA, highly conscious of those goals, will have scheduled him meticulously, researched and prepared the necessary briefing materials, arranged for timely departure and transportation, prepared the way for his smooth reception at the destination, and attended to every detail essential for the success of her boss's endeavor.

Powerful stereotypes exist. Geniuses and visionaries are messy and disorganized. Orderliness is a waste of time, and being organized is a sign of a plodding and uncreative mind. Whether these stereotypes are true or not, I have encountered a few stereotypically disorganized yet powerful and effective leaders who trust their assistants to complement their leadership qualities and offset their weaknesses.

For levity's sake, some examples of clichéd disorganization at the leadership level:

- Messy desk syndrome—paper upon paper, file upon file, so items on the bottom of the pile are lost forever. And cluttered office syndrome—sometimes exacerbated by the inability to throw anything away. The assistant will have a foolproof electronic filing system that keeps track of every paper document before it reaches the boss's desk or office.

- The executive should copy electronic documents that might slip through the above system to the assistant, or she should have access to the boss's e-mail to retrieve them and file them for future reference. (The second option is more trustworthy.)

- Every electronic document is stored on the boss's computer desktop until he gets blurry-eyed trying to find anything. The assistant will offer to organize the desktop into subject files so like can be filed with like, at the very least.

- "If I give you this document to file, what happens if you are sick and I can't find it when I need it? I'll just keep it in my office." Though the offer is unlikely to be accepted, the assistant could, theoretically, teach the boss the office filing system. In these times, it is likely to be electronic and therefore accessible from anywhere.

- "What am I supposed to do, and where am I supposed to be next?" typifies the executive who focuses intently on the task of the moment or the person she is currently meeting but loses track of long-range plans or schedules. This behavior is a challenge because the assistant must continuously watch the clock to keep her boss on time and has little opportunity to focus on work that needs her full attention.

- "Your desk is so clean and tidy. Do you need more work?" The misconception that those who are well-organized and neat are not busy when the opposite is most often true!

Some may accuse me of being judgmental for depicting one person as organized and another as disorganized. Who am I to decide whether one work style or habit is problematic and needs complementing? There is a common perception that brilliant people are disorganized in their living and working habits; they become so absorbed with creative and innovative ideas that neatness and orderliness simply get in their way. I cannot say if this leadership style is anything more than a myth, but I maintain that such a leader would benefit from an EA who is an accomplished organizer.

Of course, complementarity, in its purest form, goes

both ways. In the EA, the executive should foster the leadership skills that make possible her promotion to more and more responsible roles. Let us not lose sight of the full meaning of complementary: "combining in such a way as to enhance or emphasize the qualities of each other."

VI. DISRESPECT AND HUMILITY

When I told some of my former colleagues, the EAs I worked with during my Harvard career, that I intended to write about executive assistants and respect, a couple of them told me stories.

Most said that they have a very respectful partnership with their executives but that gaining the respect of others in the organization, particularly those who report directly to their executive, is frequently difficult, at times frustrating, and, in some cases, a failure.

I admit that I don't fully understand it because I haven't been in the shoes of those who do not respect their bosses' assistants. Trying to put myself in such direct reports' shoes, I imagine that they see the EAs as barriers between themselves and their bosses. The EA may hinder direct access when they want unfettered entry to the executive's space, time, and hearing. They bristle at a go-between passing messages: She might get it wrong. They are sure that she can't possibly understand the urgency or full context of their need. They want her out of the way so they can get their requests answered instantaneously. Or they haven't gotten what they wanted from their boss in the past, and they suspect it is the EA's fault. If the assistant reads her boss's e-mail, they may feel deprived of the privacy and intimacy they imagine would exist if she were not always the observer.

Do you notice that my tone in the above paragraph belies my lack of understanding of the direct report's perspective? I'm having difficulty getting into their shoes. Precisely that is the cause of disrespect in many situations—the unwillingness or inability to see the problem from the other's point of view.

The truth is, in many cases, the executive has asked her EA to be a doorkeeper in general, and in *particular* for specific individuals. This responsibility may create an awkward state of affairs because the boss wants her to do so without the slightest hint that the executive has instituted the practice. The EA must take the flack and the disrespect with equanimity.

The EA is sometimes disrespected in relationships with EAs of executives further up in the hierarchy. A pecking order does exist! "My boss is more important than your boss, so I don't have to be polite to you. I can demand whatever I need," may be the attitude of EAs at the top level. Perhaps they don't express such blatant contempt, but rather a subtle lack of respect. Wise assistants at any level will work hard to build respectful relationships with their peers and those up and down the hierarchy. They know it's the best way to accomplish what they should all want to achieve—smooth and efficient interactions in the interest of their bosses' success. More crudely expressed, it's, "You scratch my back, and I'll scratch yours," with a modicum of grace and humor added to the mix.

What about the individuals in the organization who exhibit poor interpersonal skills (including lack of respect) with everyone? In those instances, the EA may become the tutor and mentor, encouraging a more respectful, softer touch in the interest of the other's career and the organization's benefit. Since the assistant is on the front lines, she may take the brunt of much rudeness and learn not to take it personally. She will try to turn the situation around and advise on the best way to accomplish a task without ruffling feathers. But she is not a doormat. She will not allow rude behavior to become the norm for the staff's interactions with her. She is called upon to model and describe the acceptable and effective behavior that will help others accomplish their goals.

EAs often experience a sort of generalized disrespect because some of them don't have college or higher degrees and are therefore considered "a dime a dozen." Some may deem them unambitious because they have not focused on upward mobility. They love their work and are happy to make a career of being executive assistants. Those who want to play that role impeccably are avid about professional development and continuous learning, but they do not want to go back to school to get a PhD. They are always honing their technical and interpersonal skills and are enthusiastic about taking on new challenges. The EA's best tools for countering the "dime a dozen" mentality are self-knowledge, self-acceptance, and self-respect—realistic humility.

I don't mean to paint all EAs as exemplary and all those who do not respect them as unfair and self-interested. Of course, there are situations in which esteem is not earned or deserved. In those instances, the respectful course of action would be to speak directly to the EA about the problems experienced. If improvement does not occur, then discussing the issues with the assistant's boss is both appropriate and respectful.

Capable EAs are the oil that lubricates the whole organization, and the best ones both know it and are known for it!

VII. POLITICAL SAVVY AND DIPLOMACY

I 've touched on both political awareness and diplomacy in several previous chapters, but I will write about them more directly in this one. What am I talking about when I commend them as qualities of a competent and respected executive assistant?

An article entitled "Political Savvy in the Office: What It Really Means" from the website Success Labs gives an apt description of the kind of savvy an EA should seek to develop.

> At its core, **political savvy** is simply a deep under-
> standing of what other people need, born of em-
> pathy, listening, and honest communication... Pol-
> itical savvy can get a bad reputation. Too often, it
> can conjure up images of backstabbing coworkers
> and up-and-comers who stop at nothing to get
> to the top... Political savvy reflects [the] ability to
> understand the [work] environment. People some-
> times shy away from developing political savvy.
> They may not want to be seen as a "plotter" or
> "fake"... But in any workplace, nothing is black and
> white—there's always ambiguity, unwritten rules,
> and different personalities to deal with. You need
> political savvy to deal with those personalities and
> rules... [Political Savvy in the Office: What It Really
> Means; Success Labs (mysuccesslab.com)]

In politics and business, it is fashionable to look for
"outsiders" to fill various roles and bring new perspectives to the table. While there may be merit in such
an approach, and fresh ideas are valuable in any organization, I'm usually attracted to the more experienced
insiders, provided they are not jaded and manipulative,
and they demonstrate political savvy. They are the ones
who know all the players and their habits and tricks, the
ones who know who can and will help them to advance
a cause, who to avoid, and with whom to seek closer
relationships.

Political savvy and diplomacy form a tightly woven

cloth. The art of dealing with people sensitively and effectively, *diplomacy*'s synonyms describe the kind of person everyone wants as a colleague: one who acts with tactfulness, discretion, subtlety, finesse, delicacy, savoir-faire, politeness, thoughtfulness, care, judiciousness, and prudence.

With these understandings of political savvy and diplomacy, let me turn to an example of them in an EA's work. Suppose the executive gives his assistant a delicate task to complete, requiring perfect timing, confidentiality, teamwork, and an optimal outcome in a complicated situation. Let's say he asks her to place an important and controversial report, already vetted by the CEO, in the organization's communications officer's hands. The head of the company is holding her boss, the author of the report, responsible for a public release that will paint the organization in the best possible light. Her boss is in Asia; they have had extensive phone conversations about publishing the report, but he believes a face-to-face delivery to the communications director is optimal. His EA must stand in for him.

The EA must know how the communications office works and how much confidentiality to expect from it before publication. Can rumors or leaks be anticipated? How can she and the communications director head them off? She must already have a trusting relationship with the director, and a clear understanding of how he operates in such situations will be essential. How should the report be delivered, and with what caveats? Does the EA command enough respect in the communications office to be accepted as a stand-in representing her boss's concerns with authority, subtlety, and tact? Are there any pitfalls that she has encountered before that she must avoid in this instance? The release's timing is critical, and she must negotiate it with an understanding of the director's constraints and concerns. She must be ready to respond to questions from a nuanced grasp of her boss's values, views, and goals. She must function as an ambassador and a diplomat. She will shepherd this matter to its successful conclusion acting as a liaison between the CEO, her boss, and the communications office. Who should she avoid, who should she engage? Who should she stand up to, and when should she acquiesce?

Admittedly, in this situation, the number of players is limited, and they are well known to each other. However, other industry news outlets and the public media will also be involved. Other EAs will read their bosses' e-mails or merely overhear phone conversations. The intricacy of the task emerges, and the delicacy required is apparent.

So, let's step back. Who would you rather have in the center of this complex hub? An outsider, new to the organization, or a seasoned, politically savvy, and diplomatic executive assistant? You do not want her to be manipulative or self-serving, insensitive or indiscreet, and certainly not uninformed and bumbling.

The EA who maintains a low profile, operates in the background, keeps her eyes and ears open, and synthesizes all the information, cues, and motives swirling around her can steer a straight (or, if necessary, convoluted) path to the goal.

A place for innocence and inexperience exists in every organization. An executive may choose to hire such an EA to train her to fulfill his support needs in the unique fashion that best suits him. The goal of the novice EA, however, must be to become politically savvy and diplomatic. She should not scorn her more experienced role models but observe their grace and wisdom in complex situations and be ready for the day she will be required to become a diplomat herself.

VIII. FAILURE

"**F**ail, fail again, fail better."
—*Pema Chödrön, Buddhist Monastic*

When Naropa University accepted Pema Chödrön's granddaughter, the nun promised she would speak at the young woman's commencement ceremony. Her address, later published as a small book entitled *Fail, Fail Again, Fail Better*, was based on a quote from Samuel Beckett, the Irish author: "Ever tried, ever failed? No matter. Try again. Fail again. Fail better."

Do Pema Chödrön and Samuel Beckett glorify failure?

What do they mean, fail once, fail again, and fail better? Isn't once enough? Isn't failing again, especially at the same task or enterprise, demonstrating incompetence, stupidity, or the inability to learn from one's mistakes? And how can you pair the words *fail* and *better*? Isn't that pairing an oxymoron?

I could not continue to write about respect and the executive assistant without mentioning that all EAs, even the best of us, are human. Failure, on occasion, is inevitable for everyone. Some failures lead to catastrophic events in our lives: dismissal from a job, the end of a marriage, the loss of esteem from those we love most. Such enormous failures may leave us broken, consumed by guilt, and wondering if there is a way to go on, to go forward. Other shortcomings are less consequential, merely embarrassing, and may leave us wondering about our competence and worth.

Like everyone else, the mature, balanced, and self-composed EA is not devastated by her mistakes and failures —small or large. She knows that they are events in the flow of her work life and not a descriptor of her as a person. Every failure is an opportunity to learn. When the EA finds herself in a vortex of negligence, oversight, or carelessness of her own making, she will first ask herself, "How can I get through this?" And second, "What can I learn from it?" She might also say, "How can I make sure I don't fail again?" but this is an unrealistic hope. Failure is part of the fabric of life; hence, "Fail, fail again, fail better."

A few excerpts from Pema Chödrön's commencement address at Naropa may shed light on the concept of "failing better."

[James] Joyce wrote about how failure can lead to discovery. And he actually didn't use the word "failure"; he used the word "mistake," as in making a mistake. He said that mistakes can be "the portals of discovery." In other words, mistakes are the portal to creativity, to learning something new, to having a fresh look on things [p.45]... Can you allow yourself to feel what you feel when things don't go the way you want them to [?] (p.61)... "Fail better" means you begin to have the ability to hold the rawness of vulnerability in your heart and see it as your connection with other human beings and as a part of your humanness (p.115)... Failing better means that failure becomes a rich and fertile ground instead of just another slap in the face (p.116). (*Fail, Fail Again, Fail Better*, Pema Chödrön, Sounds True, 2015)

How does the executive assistant feel when her carefully constructed and meticulously detailed travel itinerary, the hundredth she has created, is missing a crucial piece of information? The oversight causes her boss to call, in a panic, from Los Angeles airport on his way to Japan to say he has no seat assignment. How does she feel, and what does she do when her executive calls, furious, from downtown saying that the meeting on the calendar for two p.m. was over before she arrived? What will the EA say? What kinds of checks and balances will she initiate for the future? Will her self-confidence take a nosedive? How does she recover and move forward? What if, in a momentary lapse of caution, she reveals a confidence? Or a report is published containing errors that embarrass her manager? What if she commits a cultural faux pas while welcoming high-profile international guests, offending the visitors?

I could go on and on with examples of common mistakes and failures. Virtually every EA I know can find herself somewhere in the above list of omissions or missteps. The brave ones call on deep reserves of humility and fine-tuned grace to recover quickly and correct the situation. They own up to the mistake, take responsibility for it, apologize, and describe how they plan to avoid it in the future. They do not spend time wallowing in guilt, shame, and blame, knowing these emotions do not help them or the others involved. They respect their larger, fuller personas, and they offer the same understanding and respect to others when they fail.

I want to emphasize the invaluable practice of self-respect. Saying that you respect yourself while sitting quietly and reflecting on what about you is respectable is all well and good. Practicing self-respect under challenging conditions, when your actions are unsuccessful or less than optimal, is another matter entirely. Refusing to listen to the inner voices of blame or to get stuck in the self-accusation of failure takes strength and practice. You are bigger than the current fiasco. Your identity is broader, fuller, more comprehensive than the bungled incident at hand. So, do not waste energy pasting a "failure" label on your forehead; focus on what to do now and then reflect on what you might do in similar situations in the future. Failing better takes practice, and you will learn to see it as a "portal to creativity."

The principle of "nonidentification" is a hard one to grasp and practice. Refuse to allow the small persona of the momentary failure to train-wreck your larger persona—who you are at the core and in the bigger perspective of your life. To practice successfully, you must be honest with yourself but eschew self-judgment. Breathe deeply, calm the embarrassment and self-recriminations, find a quiet place and time to get in touch with the roots of your distress and shame, stay in this inner space, and be kind to yourself. Allow yourself to accept your humanness and essential goodness. Celebrate it! And then, go forth and "Fail, fail again, fail better!"

IX. RELIABILITY AND LOYALTY

I have saved the least glamorous traits of an accomplished EA for late in this book. They are the bedrock of her relationship with her executive. Occasional brilliance is welcome, but reliability is essential. Disloyalty is flagrant, but loyalty is a quiet and hidden jewel.

When I retired from Harvard, my school threw me a retirement party. I was blown away, as they say, by the number and diversity of those who attended. I was honored by the presence of the five deans I had served in the last 15 years of my career there and by the way they described my service. I was touched and happy that the guests included other assistants and program managers, custodial staff, and colleagues and leaders from across the university.

When my former bosses spoke about the kind of service I offered them, the word *reliable* came up repeatedly. What memories did that word conjure in their minds as they spoke? I imagine they remembered that I was in the office before they were on many mornings and sometimes still there when they left at night. They could count on me doing my best to make it to the office on snowy winter days when the university remained open and, if I couldn't get there, to work and be available from home. They knew that if I felt sick, I would try to rise above it and come to work anyway if some crucial tasks or events needed attention. If I were so ill I couldn't "rise above it," they relied on me to arrange for coverage from among the team of assistants with whom I worked closely. They knew I would not drop any task balls in play. They would not be left high and dry, embarrassed, or unprepared. Deadlines would still be met, projects would be on track, and deliverables delivered.

Of course, I was not perfect. Sometimes, at hectic times, something would slip through the cracks. Over the years, I had learned to minimize these omissions by setting up systems to check and double-check myself. And when something did slip through this fine sieve of backup techniques, I had learned not to freak out but remain calm and fix the problem quickly.

They all knew I "had their backs," which brings me to loyalty. In a real EA/executive partnership, the boss is not paying only for all the qualities I've discussed in previous chapters—prescience, discretion, humor, stability, political savvy, diplomacy, and humility—but is also investing in a strong bond of allegiance or loyalty. The executive may not have realized that loyalty is a two-way street, but she certainly wants it coming in her direction.

I made it a practice—no, a policy—never to discuss an executive with his successor. During my last executive assistant role, executives came and went. While I passed on to each new one the lessons their predecessors and I had learned, I never spoke about the personality, strengths and weaknesses, victories, or screw-ups of those who had come before. We only talked in the most general terms of insights gained or disappointments that turned into learning experiences. Because I didn't break confidences from one executive to another, I assume they concluded I would be loyal to them each in turn. I was.

Sometimes I watched the reputation of my young EA colleagues' reliability falter on the mistake of many sick days taken in short periods; on lateness, ball-dropping, confidence-breaking, and careless mistakes. And sometimes I watched them soar as they grew in expertise, maturity, wisdom, reliability, and loyalty. And I celebrated with pride in my heart the careers they were launching, the growing responsibilities they would assume, and the excellent references they would receive as they moved forward.

My EA colleagues were a dedicated, brilliant, and versatile lot. I hope they knew, in their hearts, their worth to their bosses and to the organization they served.

X. MULTITASKING AND MINDFULNESS

W hat is multitasking?

Multitasking, in a human context, is the practice of doing multiple things simultaneously, such as editing a document or responding to e-mail while attending a teleconference. [What is multitasking (in humans)? - Definition from WhatIs.com (techtarget.com)]

What is mindfulness?

"Mindfulness" can be defined as being conscious and aware. It really is about being present in the moment and focusing your attention on what's at hand. ("Why you should choose mindfulness over multitasking," by Sarah Wall, April 4, 2019, open-source.com)

Requirements for multitasking in EA job descriptions are ubiquitous. We are all required in everyday work and personal life to pay attention to many things simultaneously. I don't take issue with this fact of life.

Research, however, has shown that multitasking is both inefficient and fatiguing for the brain. Author Daniel Goleman, in his book, *Focus: The Hidden Driver of Excellence* (New York, Harper Collins, 2013, p. 203), points out that "routine disruptions from a given focus at work can mean minutes lost to the original task. It can take ten or fifteen minutes to regain full focus." Continuous "switch-tasking," a more accurate descriptor for the daily work patterns of many EAs, is stressful for both the brain and the body.

Sarah Wall describes a study on multitasking in her April 2019 article:

In a study, self-described multitaskers were asked to switch back and forth between tasks at a pace that felt natural to them. A control group was asked to do one job at a time in sequence. The multitasking group performed far less effectively. Each time

49

they switched tasks, there was a slowdown because it took time to recall the details and the steps they'd done so far. This wound up making everything take roughly 40% longer ("Multitasking: Switching Costs: Subtle 'switching' costs cut efficiency, raise risk." American Psychological Association, March 20, 2006) and led to lower levels of accuracy overall. People who focused on one task at a time spent less time overall and finished all the tasks.

She goes on to say:

The mind functions optimally when it can focus on one activity at a time. Choosing mindfulness over multitasking will result in better feelings throughout your day and help you do better work... There are many advantages to mindfulness in the workplace. The trick is creating boundaries and habits that allow you to give each task your full attention.

Creating boundaries and habits is, indeed, the trick. Most EAs work in an environment that makes them highly interruptible. They are often on the front line of funneling requests to their bosses, and therefore must be available to all those who interact with their executives. Finding time to focus is difficult, and on some occasions, impossible. It will undoubtedly help the EA if her boss understands this dynamic and supports her in setting aside uninterrupted time to focus on substantial projects.

The volume of work can also be a barrier to mindful practice in the workplace. I have sometimes talked myself down off the ledge of panic when faced with too many projects by telling myself to pick up the first piece of paper that comes to hand and give it my full attention until I accomplish its task. I have suggested this method to others, and they have also found it helpful. It relieves stress and builds confidence and momentum.

Setting aside time during a workday to approach a project mindfully is so challenging that many EAs and their principals arrive at the office before business hours to find some "quiet" to think and work. Others work evenings and weekends. Working from home has become an accepted way to achieve concentration. Away from the office's constant interruptions, many can be more creative, disciplined, and productive.

I write about mindfulness related to EAs because, at present, "single-tasking" or "serial-tasking" is still bucking the prevailing wind. Some think that an executive's or leader's higher-level functions may require mindful attention, but those of his EA do not. This is simply not true. Close your door, let the phone go to voice mail, don't open your e-mail account, and take a few deep breaths. It will do wonders for your ability to bring any vital project to completion.

XI. DUAL REPORTS

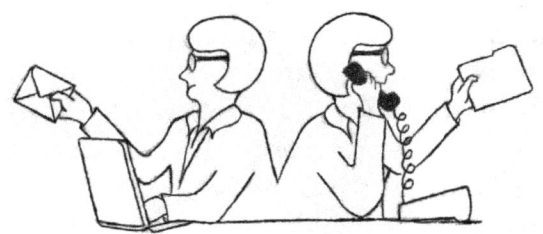

A "dual reporting" relationship is one in which an employee reports to two managers. In some situations, "multi-reporting" is practiced to address several managers' support needs by appointing one assistant. The organization may save wage and benefit dollars, but I have seldom seen such an arrangement work to the advantage of either managers or employees. With the best of intentions, bosses will agree, in principle, to share their support staff, but in practice, each of them will insist that his or her requests receive top priority. It is then left to the assistant to juggle multiple tasks, perhaps more than a workweek can accommodate, while trying to please all her managers.

Like multitasking, dual reporting is a practice that I believe is doomed to failure in most situations. Indeed, it can be a way of setting up a perfectly competent person to fail at her job. She may be a whiz at calculating priorities, but her calculations may not meet the expectations of both her bosses. The net effect will be frustration for all parties, competition among managers, and overwork for the EA involved.

Sometimes the desire or the pressure to save money plays havoc with human resource best practices, and downright unachievable expectations are inserted into a job posting. HR departments may have incomplete knowledge of the day-to-day responsibilities they are aggregating in one position description. Sometimes bosses are not consulted thoroughly or at all about their support needs. Sometimes they are pressured to consent to a dual-reporting hire due to budget concerns. The unsuspecting applicant may enter a situation that may, ultimately, be unworkable for everyone.

I will not belabor this point. Be extremely careful when entering a dual reporting relationship. Make the managers and the organization's human resource office aware up-front if you have concerns about establishing priorities, meeting everyone's expectations, and the possibility of overwork before you accept the position. Quiz them about their openness to reconsidering the structure of the job after a period of initiation. Foster a practice of open communication between all parties regularly. Bosses and HR officers, please welcome the insight of the person you are hiring as the EA, especially an experienced one. She does not want to let anyone down.

XII. THE VACATION DILEMMA

At a particular time in my career, I began to dread vacations. Though my body and mind acknowledged the need to get away from work to renew and refresh, doing so was often more exhausting and stressful than staying in the office.

When a relationship between the executive and his assistant is, in the fullest sense, a collaboration and a partnership, it's hard to plug in a temp or even an in-house replacement for the EA on vacation. When expert knowledge and wisdom are vital in a role, it can seem foolhardy to leave the office unstaffed for two weeks or in the hands of someone without the requisite background understanding.

In such cases, the EA will often spend extra hours outside the typical workday preparing for her time away, ensuring that everything she can anticipate is in place for the office's smooth operation. Such work typically goes unnoticed. She may also spend time training a temporary replacement, though such a solution is only partial because a temp cannot do more than the most basic tasks.

While away "on vacation," the EA may feel it is necessary to read her own and her boss's e-mail in an attempt to maintain the contextual knowledge needed for her to hit the ground running upon her return. She may stay up late or rise early while away, trying to stay in touch with what is going on at work.

No matter how much effort she puts into keeping track of work activities and decisions while away, upon her return, she will have to weed through reams of e-mails and figure out which still require action or whether the actions taken in her absence need review and correction. She must also take care of the tasks her boss did not feel comfortable assigning to her temporary replacement. She will probably do so outside of office hours because the daily work engine is still barreling along at full speed. All this extra work is why EAs sometimes have more accrued vacation than they feel comfortable using.

Is a real vacation an unsolvable dilemma? I have thought so for much of my EA career. Only now, after several years of retirement, do I find myself approaching an inkling of a solution. A quote from the Persian poet Rumi holds a clue: "Never give from the depths of your well, but from your overflow." One of the crudest interpretations of this quote is that what you dredge up from the bottom of your energy supply is unlikely to be the best you want to give to your job.

When I was in my thirties, I lived in an area of the country near several lakes. The early fall would bring flocks of Canada geese to these stopover bodies of water on their flight to warmer climates. Their V-shaped formation as they took off from the water and flew out of sight fascinated me. A sentence sprang to my mind without any conscious thought: "Formation is for long-distance flying."

Remember, you are engaged in a long-distance journey. Make sure you observe aerodynamic principles: Rely on the strength and expertise of the whole flock, drop back to catch your breath and recoup when necessary, move to the front of the formation when you are feeling renewed and vigorous. Acknowledge that you cannot make this journey alone.

If the job is too big for the person who holds it to take a vacation, then perhaps two people should be sharing the job, or management should consider adding a second position!

XIII.
DISAPPOINTMENT

Now I will touch on the situations in an executive assistant's life that disappoint and cause heartache.

Occasionally, at Harvard, EAs who supported deans across the university would gather for a "retreat day" or an "off-site," a day together, away from their offices, to encourage each other, share experiences and lessons learned, and hear from an expert in some aspect of higher education. These days were few but treasured. Few because getting away from our desks was such an enormous undertaking. Yes, we could arrange our work plans to make time available, but we didn't work according to *our* schedules, but our bosses' and their teams'. We treasured the off-sites because they assuaged the isolation we sometimes felt, wondering if anyone else understood our concerns, problems, and yes, even our victories.

At one of these retreats, I happened to be part of a small group whose members included the EA from one of the most prestigious graduate schools. Her boss had recently been appointed to a leadership role in a renowned higher education institution and had invited the EA to move with her. The assistant felt honored. Her life circumstances made it possible for her to accept, and so she did. She talked about the partnership she and her boss had developed over the years. She commented on conversations they had at the end of many days, reflecting together on issues and how to resolve them. She said that her boss was always open to her perspective, bounced ideas off her, and valued her judgment and input. The EA looked forward to the same kind of relationship as they faced this new challenge together.

We, her colleagues, rejoiced with her. Congratulations flowed like wine, and it was a very lively small-group discussion. Reflecting afterward, though, I felt sure this kind of partnership was rare. I have lost track of this EA over the years, so I don't know how things went as she and her principal settled into their new roles. Perhaps in a different setting, the partnership was harder to sustain. I hope not.

Many EAs have poured out their energies, insights, and hearts to support executives who do not value the treasure they have. The executives are glad that the office runs smoothly, projects are completed, and their needs are anticipated and met. But they never give a thought to the effort expended behind the scenes during the workday, late at night, or on weekends to accomplish these feats. They don't recognize the wisdom and dedication their EA brings to the enterprise. One of the most demoralizing experiences for an EA is knowing that her boss doesn't know (or care) what she is doing to perform the miracle he or she requires.

A gift from his travels, a remembered birthday or special occasion, faithful thank-you's don't touch that place in the heart of a dedicated, hardworking, insightful, and wise EA who longs to partner with her executive. What would be her real reward? To be consulted about projects, have her advice and insight sought, and be treated as a valued problem-solver and an integral part of the executive team. In other words, to be a partner in the endeavor at hand, not a servant, no matter how relied upon and appreciated that servant might be.

My advice to all bosses would be to look up and around you, recognize your assistant's potential, and seize the opportunity to foster a close and mutually beneficial relationship that will serve your goal, your EA's goal, and the good of your organization. Nurture, support, and grow your partner. Invest in her as she invests in you. Consider your EA an invaluable resource and treat him or her as such. You will never regret it.

XIV. THE FAILED PARTNERSHIP

A partnership is an association of two or more people as partners. Synonyms for partnership include cooperation, collaboration, coalition, and alliance.

Few circumstances are more disappointing in an executive assistant's career than to enter into a relationship that she believes will be a working partnership, only to discover that the executive does not understand what partnership means and is incapable of building or sustaining it. Of course, the same disappointment may occur for the executive.

The EA does not expect a professional partnership with her boss to be an equal one. The executive is the employer, and the EA, the employee. A natural imbalance of power is built into the relationship. However, if the two are to create an effective two-person "collaboration" or team, a degree of partnership—characterized by mutual respect, trust, reliability, and even friendly rapport —is essential.

Starting Right

The creation of an effective partnership begins with the interview process. It is hard to learn much about a prospective partner's suitability in a series of relatively short interviews in which each party is putting the best foot forward. (Or at least one party is!)

In a world where there is a perceived glut of laborers, the power differential in an interview skews in the boss's favor. He schedules the meeting and conducts it on his turf. He has the power to hire or not and may decide the offered salary. The dynamics of the process create as much stress as possible for the interviewee. The candidate meets with a confusing series of individuals and groups, one after the other, with little transition time in between, answering the same questions multiple times. The word *marathon* is an apt descriptor for the interview process.

It may seem as if the potential boss/hiring team holds all the cards. But the prospective EA has cards as well. It's best for both parties to put as many as possible on the table during the hiring process.

EAs, try as best you can to discover the executive's work style. If you are interviewing with others on the boss's team, ask about this directly. Indeed, ask the executive herself. (It will give her a chance to self-reveal in a way that may be key to your decision about the suitability of the match.) Is the executive able to delegate? How does he do so? Is he open to suggestions from his reports? Does he seek them? Is she a visionary who hopes for an EA who will embrace and help her implement a vision? Does he like to be involved in and consulted about all project details, or is he more of a big-picture, only-if-you-hit-a-roadblock manager? Is she capable of articulating a work style and a vision?

Look around. Is his office messy or neat? Does he ask you questions during the interview, or does he talk only about himself, his needs, and those of the organization? Is she passionate about the goals of the organization and her role in it? Does he seem interested in your career development? Is he willing to go to bat for a fair salary? How hard does she work? What is her work–life balance, and what are her expectations of her EA in this regard? If he is likely to value a true partnership with his executive assistant, he will not be put off by such questions. He will know how important they are in establishing a partnership.

Of course, each party comes out of an interview process with only a limited amount of information. The reliability of first impressions will depend upon how open and honest both parties have been.

I interviewed for a job four times during my EA career. During all but one of these interviews, the hiring manager monopolized the conversation. He or she used the meeting to describe the position, the organization, and its needs. He or she seemed to have given my résumé a cursory glance and to be uninterested in learning more about me or asking probing questions to determine what I might have to offer.

In the best interview, the interviewer (who was not the executive herself) asked very complex hypothetical questions about how I might handle certain situations that were likely to arise while assisting the executive with whom I would work. By the end of the interview, I had a good idea of what I might be getting myself into and the kind of relationship I might have with my new boss. And the interviewer had a fuller picture of how I was likely to react in various real-life circumstances and whether my reactions would suit the executive with whom I would be working.

Sometimes lower-level managers—human resource (HR) departments and office administrators—make the hiring decisions, with the executive simply giving a final blessing to a candidate recommended by the staff. Depending upon the HR hiring officer (and the salary and personnel constraints under which HR is operating), the executive's and EA's compatibility may or may not receive its due weight. Indeed, if you find yourself offered an EA position with an executive whom you have hardly met, the chances are very slim that he is looking for a true partner.

Several times during my EA career, my bosses inherited me from their predecessors. I knew the office's circumstances, the team members' personalities and skills, my new boss's job description, and the organization's goals better than he or she. Therefore, I was in a stronger position to demonstrate how my skills and talents could add value to their work lives and position myself for a working partnership.

All of this is to say that the seeds of a true partnership are sown during the interview process. The EA who wants to partner with her boss should not be shy about demonstrating a "partnership" attitude or speaking openly of her hopes to develop such a relationship for the good of the office and the organization. Suppose this attitude and the open expression of her hopes are rebuffed or ignored by the hiring executive. In that case, the chances are good that her efforts to build a productive partnership later on will be frustrated.

Let me not be pie-in-the-sky about the interview process. In most workplaces in the present employment climate, management expects employees to do more and more for less and less salary, with longer hours and shrinking benefits. Any job with any boss may seem more attractive than unemployment. You may need to "settle."

Developing the Partnership

If the hiring executive has demonstrated clear signs that he wants to work together as partners, both he and the EA will start building such a relationship immediately. Their "check-in" time together (daily, if possible, except when the boss is traveling) will be held sacrosanct. It will be a well-organized exchange of information in a streamlined and efficient manner. It is primarily the EA's responsibility to schedule, plan, and conduct these check-ins. Each will listen deeply to the other, learn essential details about every agenda topic, and study the other's reactions, ways of thinking, values, concerns, and priorities. The EA knows her executive will make decisions without seeking her input in many instances, but still, she will feel comfortable offering her views and expects her boss to value them.

Red flags should go up for the EA if the executive routinely cancels these check-ins, isn't willing to listen when she has a viewpoint to offer, or seems uninterested in her concerns. They both recognize that in a true partnership, the executive will feel comfortable sharing confidential business information with his assistant. They both know that the EA can handle situations more professionally and effectively if she has the complete picture.

The executive must understand that the EA needs uninterrupted time to accomplish tasks and projects that require extended periods of focused thought, and he will ensure such time is available. The executive will also know that an assignment that may seem relatively simple and quick to accomplish might take much longer than he imagines. Though many tasks are invisible to him, he trusts his EA to take all the hidden steps, jump through all the secret hoops, and exchange behind-the-scenes e-mails. He may be happy in his ignorance, but he is solid in his trust.

Failed Partnerships – Some Scenarios

ONE

Cindy walks into her boss Jay's office soon after he assumes his new responsibilities with the company that she has served for six years. She and Jay have read a series of e-mails from others complaining about a problematic employee who reports directly to him. Suspecting that Jay may not have a complete picture of the situation and wanting to help him deal with it effectively, she says, "May I offer some information and a suggestion—?" Jay cuts her off, responding, "No." Cindy is dismayed but hides her reaction and leaves the office to process what has just happened.

Her interactions with Jay up to that point have been positive. Of course, she will give him the benefit of the doubt but will, in the future, carefully choose those moments when she offers an opinion or a suggestion. Over the next few months, her observations of and interactions with Jay confirm her early impression. He is not open to her ideas, does not value her input, and prefers to use her as a clerical secretary. He is insecure enough to believe he must have all the answers and make all the decisions unaided by her experience. Others in the company are whispering about similar interactions with Jay.

TWO

Deborah hired Naomi with great fanfare and good will. She liked Naomi's professional manner, her energy, her self-assurance, and her extensive experience. They each felt an immediate rapport. Naomi proved competent, reliable, and a good problem-solver in the first months of their work together. She usually came to Deborah to report how she had headed off a problematic issue rather than dump the problem in Deborah's lap.

For her part, Naomi felt trust growing between herself and Deborah. She felt respected and valued. But about nine months into their partnership, Deborah made a business decision that shocked and disappointed Naomi. She thought long and hard about all Deborah's possible motives, trying to understand what had brought her to this decision. Finally, Naomi decided to talk with Deborah directly about her discomfort and offer her perspective on the injustice the decision had created. She hoped that their conversation would help her understand Deborah's perspective and that Deborah might change her mind.

Deborah listened to Naomi's views and offered reasons for her decision, but Naomi did not believe those reasons were justified or valid. She left the meeting feeling that Deborah was blind to the injustice she had caused. Naomi struggled with her convictions, sought counsel from trusted friends, and ultimately decided she must resign from her post. Her values were incompatible with Deborah's on this matter. She believed that their promising partnership could not sustain this incompatibility and had foundered on opposing values. Deborah was sorry to lose Naomi but understood the strength of her EA's feelings and respected Naomi's commitment to her principles. They parted, saddened but understanding each other's perspectives.

THREE

Richard respected those who worked for him. He said openly and frequently that he could not do his job without the skilled, loyal, dependable staff who effectively supported him and the organization. He took an interest in their career development, offered them opportunities for continuing education, and understood their needs for flexible schedules and a healthy work–life balance. Richard was proud of staff members when they moved on from his department to higher organizational levels and more challenging work. The professional growth of his EA, Alex, was exceptionally gratifying. He had hired him as a temp fresh out of college, had seen his potential, and had promoted him to be his executive assistant. He trusted Alex completely, and Alex didn't disappoint.

They worked together happily and productively for eight years. Though he didn't carry the title, in many ways, Alex functioned as Richard's chief of staff, making the whole department run more smoothly. They understood each other perfectly, Richard thought. Alex could anticipate his unspoken needs and fulfill them. Others commented on their close partnership.

In their ninth year together, Alex started arriving late to work in the mornings. Richard ignored this, thinking that Alex would explain himself at some point and that the reason must be good. Alex worked as hard as always but began making odd errors, forgetting important but routine responsibilities. Richard tried to talk with him about the possible causes of these mistakes, but Alex said he was tired and that things would get better when he began sleeping better. Alex did not show up at work one day, leaving Richard stranded with a crucial meeting to chair. Alex had not reserved the meeting room, ordered the catered lunch, or printed and distributed materials in advance.

This was the last straw. Richard called Alex at home, exploding about his frustration and embarrassment. Alex apologized vaguely but showed up at work late again the next morning and seemed not to remember their heated call the day before. Richard called HR and asked the senior human resources officer to meet with him and Alex. The HR officer was skilled in handling such situations and created a safe space for Alex and Richard to talk about what was happening to their partnership. Alex admitted to experimenting with drugs during a time of personal loss (his father's death). The HR department recommended a treatment program, arranged medical leave, and assured Alex that his job would be waiting for him when he returned.

During Alex's leave, Richard began to fear that his and Alex's trust had eroded. He felt he had failed Alex by not noticing the depth of his mourning for his father and that Alex had failed him by not reaching out earlier to tell him what was happening. Alex struggled with embarrassment and shame and wondered how he could face Richard and work with him again. At the end of his sick leave, Alex resigned from his EA position. He and Richard said a sad farewell and eventually lost touch with each other. Alex flourished in his next job. Richard found a new EA and built a solid partnership with her. Both acknowledged that they had learned from their failed partnership.

Trust is the bedrock of any relationship. And trust is the rock on which a partnership can founder. Choose your partner carefully—eyes wide open. Trust your intuitions early on. Don't overlook signs of the relationship's instability. Invest your best energy, your best self, in developing a loyal, trusting relationship. Be clear about your values and your boundaries. Seek to understand those of your partner. Communicate and keep communicating. Accept that things change, and people change—you and your partner are no exception. Value your partnership; don't take it for granted. Do your best to strengthen it if it becomes fragile. If it fails, let go and move on but learn from the experience. Don't allow yourself to become jaded; do be careful. Invest wisely in the next partnership. Respect yourself and respect your partner.

Why is a working partnership between the EA and the executive so important? If both feel secure and draw out the best in each other in the workplace, the organization will benefit vastly.

The EA may sometimes feel misunderstood and undervalued. She works behind the scenes deriving her satisfaction from the success of others. She doesn't seek the limelight and may be embarrassed when placed in it. She doesn't consider herself a leader, but nor does she feel like a follower. She knows the value of her contributions and thrives on using her skills and wisdom to enhance her boss's accomplishments. She doesn't seek praise, but she appreciates the thankful smile, or the knowing glance, or the simple "Excellent!" now and then. The failure to achieve a partnership with her principal can be a considerable disappointment in her life and career. When respected and valued, when allowed to use all her skills and talents, experience, and wisdom, she will flourish, and so will her boss's career and the organization's mission.

XV.
TRANSITIONING
TO NEW
LEADERSHIP

Often when a new executive joins an organization, he will want to bring with him one or two team members with whom he previously worked. If that happens, those who supported his predecessor may find themselves demoted, moved to another position within the organization, or laid off. Then both the new executive and his EA will take considerably longer to orient and get up to speed in their unfamiliar jobs. Of course, they will already be a step ahead in one sense because they have worked together previously and know each other's work and management styles, strengths, weaknesses, and needs.

Suppose the executive comes alone to the new post and retains the EA for the previous leader. In that case, she will play a significant role in orienting him or her to the organization, their new position, and the staff with whom he or she will work.

I played this orientation role five times during my EA career. One must pay careful attention to several dynamics that may arise in such a situation. It may be prudent for the executive to learn the ropes and meet the team members on her own so that the EA's perceptions do not cloud the relationships that she wants to build with her new team. Or it may be helpful for the EA to alert her new boss to the pitfalls and personalities with which she is familiar due to her long tenure in the organization. Some combination of these two approaches may be the wisest choice.

I have stressed elsewhere that the EA must maintain strict confidentiality concerning the new executive's predecessor's personality and work. To build trust, the EA must refrain from criticizing her former boss or his contribution to the organization. Complaining about the office's previous situation is not professional and will not win the new executive's good will.

No new leader wants to hear unsolicited from his EA or other members of the team: "We always did it this way."

A wise and mature new executive will ask outright about past policies and whether they were effective. If he encourages such frankness, offer it without being judgmental.

That said, the EA can be the source of invaluable information about how to get things done expeditiously, who to meet first and why, and the organization's challenges and aspirations. That is if she has been encouraged by her previous boss to develop talents for political savvy, diplomacy, analysis, and confidentiality. She will introduce her new boss to the office's and organization's work systems, always open to the changes he may want to make. She will also provide relevant information on policies and organizational culture.

Good arguments exist in each situation for either staff retention or replacement during a transition to new leadership. Respect and fairness to outgoing and incoming staff will be a hallmark of the executive's reputation and success.

XVI. THE EXPENDABILITY MYTH

I n reality, of course, we are all expendable. We must be, since we are not immortal.

We should understand the definition of expendable: "of little significance when compared to an overall purpose, and therefore able to be abandoned." Some synonyms are also useful to frame the idea of expendability: dispensable, able to be sacrificed, replaceable, nonessential. (*Oxford Languages Dictionary*)

Anyone who does their job well does not fit any of the above descriptors. The most successful employers value the contributions made at every level by all members of their workforce. If they have hired smartly, if job descriptions match the necessary tasks and time required to perform them, no employee will be dispensable.

Layoffs often produce inefficiencies, overwork for those left behind, and a culture of anxiety. Even when they are essential for an organization's long-term health and financial viability, they are destabilizing and demoralizing for those who remain and those who depart.

I have included this chapter in *I've Got Your Back!* because female executive assistants are often among the first line of employees considered expendable when financial cuts are required. Indeed, they often work in an environment where management considers them replaceable because the value of their contributions is not understood. In such a milieu, they experience ongoing anxiety about their job security.

This anxiety is real for mature executive assistants who are in the middle of their careers. Years of dedication to an organization have sometimes earned them seniority, bringing a respectable and livable salary. If cuts are essential, management often assumes that hiring a younger employee to replace the senior EA will save money. (The position description is sometimes re-jiggered to make it seem like a new job for which the outgoing assistant does not qualify.) The younger EA is assumed to possess more "energy," more up-to-date technical skills, and be willing to work at a "starting level" salary.

While all these assumptions may, sometimes, be valid, there are inevitable costs to bringing a new hire up to speed. The loss of the longer-term employee's nuanced experience and wisdom may take years to recover.

Every employee works best in an atmosphere of job security. Such a workplace promotes focus, cooperation, teamwork, and creativity.

Excellence is not expendable.

XVII. TAKE CARE OF YOURSELF

This final chapter on respecting the executive assistant offers some comments on self-care. In previous chapters, you have watched me paint a picture of the ideal EA—one who is skilled, wise, reliable, poised, and extremely hardworking. You may have asked yourself, "How does this person manage to be all things to all people, still attend to her own needs, and stay mentally and physically healthy?"

My fictional "ideal" executive assistant is Blake, in *Madam Secretary*, a Netflix series chronicling a woman US Secretary of State's adventures. Blake, her assistant, is the perfect example of an EA: always one step ahead of his boss, anticipating her every need. He is integrated into her personal life, getting involved in the exploits of her husband and children (occasionally to provide levity in otherwise grim situations, and sometimes to perform the kind of salutary miracle that only a super-assistant can pull off).

Blake is "always on," always ready. His quirkiness humanizes his character. He's perpetually dressed in a suit and tie no matter the occasion, while others appear in pajamas or evening wear depending on the setting. He has a dry sense of humor, making on-target remarks and facial expressions when the camera jumps to him amid national and international crises. He even sings and plays the piano! He can get any world leader on the phone in a matter of seconds. He has his boss's coat held at the ready before she even knows she needs to exit and hands just the right report to the Secretary as she steps out of the elevator each morning. He is, of course, a caricature—one that inhabits the pinnacle of behind-the-scenes effectiveness. The Secretary trusts him completely. At least for me, their partnership is one of the most ingenious and endearing subplots of the series.

Blake is perpetually calm, self-possessed, and unflappable. Not so the EAs I have known in real life. Not so myself when I worked in this role. Behind the scenes and sometimes barely hidden in the workday, we exhibit signs of exhaustion, mental and physical overload, discouragement, frustration, anger, and the full gamut of other human emotions. Acting in a role where one is "always on" but perpetually "offstage," occupying a position where others expect you to respond with a cheerful "Come in!" whenever anyone knocks at the door, ultimately takes its toll.

The most effective executive assistants are particularly susceptible to the self-destructive habits of overwork: the inability to say no, perfectionism, and ignoring their personal needs. Like other professionals with these traits, they may burn out under prolonged stressful conditions.

In my case, the stress created by the expectations (my own and those of others) that I would be ever-efficient, continually responsive, and consistently reliable built up in my body over more than ten years until I was in almost constant pain. I decided to retire earlier than I had expected to seek relief from these physical symptoms. After retirement, I realized that stress had caused my pain, and I began an extended effort to undo the damage.

The advice I am about to offer applies to everyone but is tailored to EAs specifically. I am embarrassed, truth be told, to make suggestions that I could not implement myself when in the furnace of a stressful work atmosphere. Knowing what I know now, however, compels me to make these recommendations, embarrassing or not.

First, create work boundaries and do your best to maintain them. Don't allow them to become porous with too many exceptions. Know your limits and remember that extending them may have detrimental consequences for you and those close to you. Though it may be hard to recognize or admit, *you* will probably breach your boundaries more often than others will.

Second, know yourself well—look deeply into your motivations. Know yourself as profoundly as your well-honed insight will enable but eschew self-judging. Reflect on your work-life motives with the kindness, generosity, and self-respect that you deserve and that you would not hesitate to offer to others. Are your attitudes toward your work partially responsible for the stress and burdens you are experiencing? Must everything be done perfectly? Are you proud that you work harder than others? Do you like being the last person to turn out the lights and close the office door? Are you taking yourself and your role too seriously?

Take responsibility for your well-being. No one else will "fix" or rescue you from the unhealthy situations in which you find yourself. Identify what you need to feel mentally and physically healthy and courageously claim it. Be prepared that others may misunderstand or condemn your "self-protectiveness."

While creating these essential boundaries for your own sake, be kind and respectful to those who cheer and boo alike. Refrain from the habit of expecting approval or disapproval from others. Be completely up-front with your boss about the physical and emotional toll that workplace stress is taking on you. Ask if he or she will brainstorm with you how to change the work situation for the better for both of you. If your boss does not understand your needs or support your decision to make changes in work patterns, it may be that you are not well matched as a team. You may need to sacrifice an otherwise valuable work relationship for the sake of your health.

Cultivate a physical activity that can supplement the mental gymnastics you perform during the workday. Find a creative outlet to counterbalance the routine work tasks that are essential but tedious and spirit-numbing.

Find a trusted colleague or mentor who can help you navigate challenging and sometimes toxic work situations that you may encounter. Counter the loneliness of the "secret-keeper" EA with supportive relationships outside the office. I was exceedingly fortunate during my working years to be able to confide in my life partner about situations that troubled me, knowing I could rely on her complete discretion.

Beyond all this advice, I suggest a practice that has been a healing agent in my own life—meditation. I began to practice meditation shortly after retiring as a way to ease chronic pain.

Its use to manage pain stems from the Mindfulness-Based Stress Reduction (MBSR) program. "Developed at the University of Massachusetts Medical Center in the 1970s by Professor Jon Kabat-Zinn, MBSR uses a combination of mindfulness meditation, body awareness, yoga, and exploration of patterns of behavior, thinking, feeling, and action. Mindfulness can be understood as the non-judgemental acceptance and 'open-hearted' investigation of present experience, including body sensations, internal mental states, thoughts, emotions, impulses, and memories, in order to reduce suffering or distress and to increase well-being." (Wikipedia, "Mindfulness-based stress reduction")

Meditation may involve sitting still in a comfortable position for 20 minutes (or more) while focusing attention on your breathing. The practice quiets the body and the mind, promoting relaxation, a sense of peace, and rest. Meditation is not, however, a quick panacea. Commitment, discipline, and patience are necessary to change old habits and reap new benefits. For me, the continuing effort is certainly worth it.

Regular meditation fosters mindfulness—paying attention to what is happening in the present moment with acceptance, curiosity, and compassion. Mindfulness sets us free from the inclination to create story lines in which we are victims, heroes, or saints. It wakes us up to the gift of life in the here and now. We can turn away from regrets about the past or worries about the future to live fully and gratefully in the present. I find it to be one of the best forms of self-care in the midst of demanding situations.

Everything is constantly changing, including our thoughts and feelings about our work and other parts of our lives. Mindfulness creates an openness to the flow of things, an awareness of the bigger picture. It can foster insight and can be a catalyst for change. Meditation and mindfulness calm the body and the mind and awaken curiosity, creativity, hopefulness, and courage.

A friend of mine has written a book about the impact of meditation and mindfulness practices in the workplace: *Mindfulness: A Better Me, a Better You, a Better World* by Annabel Beerel, PhD. I recommend it highly for leaders, executives, managers, and staff. The book describes mindfulness, teaches meditation, and illustrates the benefits of both. Annabel presents scientific data demonstrating the positive effect that mindfulness has on the brain and its advantages for the individual and, therefore, for the organizations in which they work. She suggests introducing it as a workplace change agent and believes that it is most effective when fostered and practiced by all workforce levels.

Meditation and mindfulness have helped me, in retirement, to deal with experiences similar to those I faced during my career as an EA: feeling overwhelmed by the number of tasks on my plate, trying to juggle and prioritize responsibilities to meet the expectations of those around me, overcommitting, rushing, attempting to multitask, catastrophizing, and failing to comprehend the bigger picture. Meditation and mindfulness have given me the courage and energy to change ineffective habits and harmful thinking patterns. They have increased my self-understanding and self-compassion and my understanding of and compassion for others.

~~~~~

I've Got Your Back! has focused on the health and well-being of EAs and the productive partnerships they create with their executives. Intrepid, they serve brilliantly behind the scenes, promoting their principals' and organizations' success. So, from the viewpoint of a retired EA, whatever nourishes your creativity, authenticity, self-respect, and compassion will make you a better EA, your boss a better executive, and your workplace a better microcosm of the world. Take care of yourself!

CONCLUSION

That's all Folks!

What you have seen in these pages, I hope, is a profound respect for a role that is frequently overlooked or undervalued.

Perhaps you sensed my urgency to convince readers, both executives <u>and</u> EAs, of the importance of this position and the people who hold it in any organization's scheme. I have seen EAs demoralized by a lack of respect and recognition. The most common disappointment is that no one understands what they do.

For instance, convening a meeting with the executive's senior staff can involve multiple e-mails or phone calls made in hierarchical order. Assistants spend hours or even days waiting for responses. EAs issue countless reminders and follow-ups. They call in favors to secure a room that accommodates the group's size and technical needs. Even if appropriate space is redundant in this era of teleconferencing or "Zooming," sometimes they coordinate across time zones. They prepare briefings sometimes tailored to each team member, smooth ruffled feelings, AND redo all these tasks patiently if something unforeseen and more important impinges on the executive's schedule.

In many places, the EA is a nonexempt employee, meaning that she is paid by the hour and not considered a professional (exempt). But professionalism is the key to her success. If she is top-notch (though she may not have an MBA or a PhD), she will demonstrate the same set of characteristics that define all professional behavior. She will exhibit "professional knowledge, proper demeanor, competency and reliability, honesty and integrity, positive attitude, [and] poise." (Skilltypes.com, "What are the six traits of professionalism?")

She may qualify for overtime when she works longer than 35 or 40 hours a week. But in many organizations, the human resource department frowns upon overtime for budgetary reasons. Many EAs do not report overtime and are not compensated for extra time spent carrying out their duties.

Even if the organization classifies an EA as an exempt, or salaried, employee, the salary may not reflect her level of expertise or the wages of male EAs with a lesser degree of experience. Profuse thanks are no substitute for earning a fair and respectable salary. I once worked for someone who displayed a sign that read, "Pay peanuts, get monkeys." When he hired me, he went to bat with the human resource administration to ensure my salary was representative of my experience and the degree of responsibility my job entailed. That gesture certainly started our partnership off on a respectful footing.

I hope both executives and executive assistants will feel that these pages reflect my respect for both. I have worked with many leaders, executives, and staff who demonstrated great integrity, talent, wisdom, and skill. I have seen true partnerships grow between EAs and their principals with all the personal and institutional rewards these relationships create.

I will close by describing a practice that I instituted in the final year of my career. Once a week, the executive assistants in my administrative area—dean, executive deans, and associate deans—gathered together. We began our meeting with a few moments of silence to allow us to detach from our busy offices, calm our physical and mental bustling, and become present to each other. Then we engaged in a round-table report-in and discussion in three parts: 1) Recent Successes;

2) Current Challenges; and 3) Office Updates. Each team member shared some accomplishments from the week just passed, a challenge they were currently facing, and finally, information from their office (schedules, projects, events) that would enhance our team's effectiveness. We refreshed our team spirit by offering each other encouragement, suggestions, and moral support. Just spending an hour with those we knew understood and respected our work helped tremendously to boost our self-esteem and restore a healthy workplace perspective.

At the end of these meetings, I came away feeling that my colleagues knew the true meaning of the promise "I've got your back!" What does it mean to "have someone's back"? You pledge to be their ally in precarious situations where they may need protection. You will be another set of eyes and ears in case they miss something. When they are busy looking ahead, you are watching from behind to ensure no one blindsides them. You will keep their well-being and success in mind and will help, underpin, and reinforce them.

It can be an enormous relief to hear, "I've got your back!" It is a bolstering promise of loyalty, support, and respect. It's what the best executive assistants offer their bosses and one another every day of their working lives.